YORK NOTES

General Editors: Professor A.N. Jeffares (*University of Stirling*) & Professor Suheil Bushrui (*American University of Beirut*)

John Millington Synge

THE PLAYBOY OF THE WESTERN WORLD

Notes by Mark Mortimer

BA (DUBLIN)
Senior Lecturer, The British Institute in Paris, Universities of London and Paris

LONGMAN YORK PRESS

YORK PRESS
Immeuble Esseily, Place Riad Solh, Beirut.

LONGMAN GROUP UK LIMITED
Longman House, Burnt Mill, Harlow,
Essex CM20 2JE, England
Associated companies, branches and representatives
throughout the world

First published 1981
Sixth impression 1993

ISBN 0-582-78278-3

Produced by Longman Singapore Publishers Pte Ltd
Printed in Singapore

Contents

Part 1

Introduction

The family background

John Millington Synge (1871–1909) was born at Rathfarnham on the outskirts of Dublin. His father was a Dublin barrister with property in Co. Galway; his mother was the daughter of a Protestant rector in Co. Cork. On both sides of the family, therefore, he belonged to what was loosely called the 'Protestant Ascendancy' class. The Synges, who had come to Ireland from England in the seventeenth century, like so many other 'planters' of similar stock, had produced a number of prominent churchmen (including five bishops) and had been wealthy landowners with property in Wicklow, Cavan, Meath and the west. The chief family estate was Glanmore Castle in Co. Wicklow, which Synge may have later described in 'A Landlord's Garden in County Wicklow'. Because of poor health, the playwright's schooling was irregular, and a lot of his time was spent wandering through the woods with a cousin called Florence Ross, collecting birds' eggs and learning about nature. This early acquaintance with the countryside, strengthened by membership of the Dublin Naturalists' Field Club and extensive walks in Wicklow during boyhood and early manhood, was to give him an unerring eye and ear for the sights and sounds of nature (there are many proofs of this in *The Playboy of the Western World*); and to provide him with a great deal of the material to be found in his writings.

A year after Synge's birth, his father died, leaving his wife to look after five children, the eldest of whom was fifteen. His upbringing was typical of many evangelical families of the time; daily prayers, absolute reliance on the Bible, strict observance of the Sabbath, avoidance of worldly activities (such as the theatre). This strict, evangelical background was reinforced by frequent summer holidays at Greystones, a fishing village twenty miles south of Dublin already growing into a holiday resort, which boasted a strong Protestant population and attracted many members of the evangelical movement as visitors.

Synge's three brothers followed careers thought appropriate for their education and class, the 'colonies', estate management, medical missions; his one sister made a 'suitable' marriage. It was left to the youngest, John, to break away from the family tradition. His first rebellion, prompted by reading Darwin, was against the evangelical faith of his family; and while he never ceased to love and honour his family, he stopped church attendance in his early teens, much to his mother's distress. He was not only endangering his soul, she felt; he was questioning the tenets of his family and class. His second reaction justified his mother's worst fears, for he rejected the social and political beliefs of the 'Ascendancy' and became a nationalist. This transformation is described in the autobiographical piece put together from notebooks, etc.:

> Soon after I had relinquished the Kingdom of God I began to take a real interest in the Kingdom of Ireland. My politics went round from a vigorous and unreasoning loyalty to a temperate Nationalism. Everything Irish became sacred . . . and had a charm that was neither quite human nor divine, rather perhaps as if I had fallen in love with a goddess . . .*

In 1888, he went to Trinity College, Dublin, and though he was never very happy or successful there, he managed to win prizes in Irish and Hebrew. Meanwhile he had taken up the study of music, with emphasis on the violin, and was turning his attention to Irish antiquities. After graduating from Trinity College with a poor degree, and taking part in several concerts, he managed, through the good offices of a cousin from England, to obtain his mother's consent to study music in Germany. However, some months there convinced him that he would never reach the level his ambition craved, so during the summer of 1894 (he was then twenty-three) he decided to give up music for writing and leave Germany for France. Unwilling to be in the second rank in the musical world, he determined to be in the first in the world of letters. He was already making terms with his declared ambition in his *Autobiography*: 'I wished to be at once Shakespeare, Beethoven and Darwin' (p.12), and directing his intellectual and artistic energies towards the realm of the first-named. His decision, once made, was irrevocable, like the earlier one to abandon the religion of his family, and the much later one to settle permanently in Ireland.

The French influence

It was natural that he should choose Paris, then the literary capital of the world; and there he was to live for fairly long periods between 1895 and 1902, spending the summer vacations in his beloved Wicklow, the county on the coast immediately south of Co. Dublin, or in the west of Ireland. Unlike the distinguished Irish men of letters who had preceded him – Oscar Wilde (1854–1900) and George Moore (1852–

*J.M. Synge, *Collected Works*, Volume II, edited by Alan Price, Oxford University Press, London, 1966, p.13.

1933) – he does not appear to have sought the company of French authors, with the single exception of Anatole Le Braz (1859–1926), the Breton regionalist writer, whose lecture on Brittany in 1897 fired his interest and influenced his reading. Synge's life in Paris was modest and obscure, a struggle (mainly unsuccessful) to achieve recognition as poet and critic, and a long quest for a personal aesthetic. Early poems, and references by those who met him in Paris, reveal poverty, loneliness and homesickness, with none of the self-assurance of a Moore or the social brilliance of a Wilde. The general impression is one of a studious, austere life, tinged with melancholy. In a poem composed in 1898 he says that his

> . . . soul is sick of the countless quais
> And the church of our Lady beyond the Seine.

However, he went frequently to concerts and plays, read widely, and attended lectures at the Sorbonne on literature and phonetics. While he seems to have been largely indifferent to French politics, he had a certain *Irish* political activity, joining the 'Association Irlandaise', founded by Maud Gonne* to promote the cause of Irish independence, and taking part in meetings and commemorative ceremonies. So, although he resigned from the 'Association' after a few months on the grounds of its 'revolutionary and semi-military character', it can be stated that his Irish political awareness, awakened by adolescent reading in Dublin and stirred by the harrowing sight of evictions in rural Ireland, was strengthened in Paris in association with dedicated nationalists, and away from the inhibitions which an Ascendancy environment might well have imposed at home. 'I wish to work in my own way for the cause of Ireland,' he said in his letter of resignation; and this may be taken as a declaration of political and cultural identity, a prophecy of his future contribution to the theatre and to literature generally.

In Paris, too, he was serving his literary apprenticeship, writing his first poems, critical articles and dramatic scraps, and thus learning to analyse and describe, criticise and construct. In this process, the example of French writers, and the discipline of the French critical method, were of incalculable assistance.

The Aran Islands

Yet despite his immense debt to France and to French literature, Synge's thoughts were constantly returning to Ireland. When he first visited the Aran Islands in 1898 (a group of islands out in the Atlantic,

*Maud Gonne was a social revolutionary, with whom W.B. Yeats fell in love in 1889. In 1903 she married John MacBride, one of the leaders executed in 1916.

to the west of Galway), there were various incentives for doing so: a family connection (an uncle, the Reverend Alexander Synge, had been Protestant incumbent there in 1851); a knowledge of the Irish language (demonstrated by the prize he won at Trinity College, and his attendance at lectures in the Sorbonne); an interest in Brittany and her culture (we recall Anatole Le Braz's lecture, and Synge's subsequent visit to the region). It is also possible that his meeting with W.B. Yeats in Paris, in 1896, was a factor in his decision, as the latter repeatedly claimed. At all events, the fact that he brought with him to the Aran Islands a copy of Pierre Loti's (1850–1923) *Pêcheur d'Islande* (1886) would suggest affinities between the two communities. Loti's description of the Breton folk and their bitter struggle with the sea, his sensitive account of the sufferings of the women who lose husbands, sons and brothers, were to be echoed in *The Aran Islands* (1907) and *Riders to the Sea* (1904).

His first visit to the Aran Islands is perhaps the most important landmark in his development as a writer. He continued to spend part of the year in Paris until 1902, but the pattern of his future, creative life in Ireland was taking shape. In the Aran Islands he found a civilisation, a setting and a people that his heart and mind responded to with love and understanding. He was to return four years running and the direct outcome of these visits is his most celebrated prose work, *The Aran Islands*. Part I of this work reflects his diffident beginnings with the spoken language (his previous knowledge of Irish was chiefly bookish); but by the time we reach Part IV, he appears to understand and speak with relative ease. Nevertheless he had no ambition to live or write in the language; it was merely a necessary vehicle for approaching a people to whom he was deeply attached.

The significance of the islands in Synge's writings goes much beyond the inspiration of his best prose work, for it was there that he found the plots of four of his six plays; and there, as he says himself, that he 'learned to write the peasant dialect and dialogue which I use in my plays'. When he finally returned to Dublin and set about dramatic composition, the period of preparation was over. The man whom Yeats later called 'the greatest dramatic genius of Ireland' was ready to make his unique contribution to the Irish theatre.

The Abbey Theatre

The opening of the Abbey Theatre in 1904 was the outcome of a combination of happy coincidence and hard work. The moving spirit behind the creation, W.B. Yeats (1865–1939), had founded in London, in 1891, the Irish Literary Society, and the National Literary Society, in Dublin, in the following year. In 1893, the Gaelic League was founded by Douglas Hyde (1862–1949)*, with the aim of reviving the Irish language and studying its existing literature: it had the effect of turning Irish people towards a noble, exciting past; of awakening a national consciousness; and of strengthening and stimulating the political movements whose goal was national independence. Oddly enough, however, the first 'Irish' plays were written in English, by writers who might be loosely termed 'Anglo-Irish'. Yeats and his friends wanted to react against the image of the 'stage Irishman', always loquacious and irresponsible, often drunken and boastful. Their manifesto stated: 'We hope to find, in Ireland, an uncorrupted and imaginative audience, trained to listen by its passion for oratory – we will show that Ireland is not the home of buffoonery and of sentiment, as it has been represented, but the home of an ancient idealism.' It was thus that an English company (there was no professional Irish company at that time) gave the first season of Anglo-Irish plays in 1899. Three years later, the Irish National Theatre Society was set up, and the Abbey opened its doors in 1904.

After the groundwork, came the happy coincidences: a wealthy Englishwoman, Miss A.E. Horniman, donated the money to buy a theatre; Lady Gregory (1859–1932), the widow of a landowner in the west of Ireland, with a close knowledge of all things Irish and a flair for the theatre, contributed her business acumen and her wise patronage; other men of letters – George Moore and Edward Martyn (1859–1923) – joined in; Yeats met the gifted amateur actors, Willie and Frank Fay; above all, a dramatist of genius appeared – J.M. Synge. Later Yeats was to sum it up very succinctly in *The Bounty of Sweden*: 'Two events brought us victory: a friend gave us a theatre, and we found a strange man of genius, John Synge.'†

The opening of the theatre was an event of great significance for Ireland, both culturally and politically. In earlier times, talented Irish dramatists – Goldsmith (1728–74) and Sheridan (1751–1816), Wilde and Shaw (1856–1950) – had taken their talents to London. Their plays were written primarily for an English audience. The themes and settings were English, the producers, actors and actresses English also. When Irish characters did appear, they were usually personifications of the 'buffoonery and sentiment' already referred to. Now, with the inauguration of the Abbey, everything had changed. Irish dramatists were encouraged, if not compelled, to write about their own country, its problems and peculiar features. The producers, actors and actresses were Irish, and the audiences that crowded the theatre were largely Irish too. Clearly such a change helped to strengthen a growing nationalism and some of the early plays – Yeat's *Cathleen na*

*The future first President of Ireland in 1937.
†W.B. Yeats, *Autobiographies*, Macmillan, London, 1955, p.556.

Houlihan (1902) is the outstanding example – were frankly vehicles for nationalist propaganda.

Synge's plays were of a very different kind. Dealing only with country people in rural settings, his work is concerned primarily with love, old age and death. His treatment of his themes and of his people is at once brutal and lyrical. He has no political or economic axe to grind. In spite of this, his first play *The Shadow of the Glen*, set in Wicklow (produced along with Yeats's *The King's Threshold* in 1903, before the Abbey was available), aroused fierce controversy on the grounds of the aspersions it was felt to cast on the absolute fidelity of Irish wives. *The Shadow of the Glen* was succeeded, in 1904, by *Riders to the Sea*, a stark one-act tragedy set in the Aran Islands. There followed *The Well of the Saints* (1905, three acts); *The Tinker's Wedding* (1908, two acts) produced in 1909; *Deirdre of the Sorrows* (three acts) published in 1910, posthumously, with a preface by Yeats and produced in the same year, with Synge's fiancée, Molly Allgood (1887–1952), in the title role. All his plays seek to recapture an imagination that, in his own words, was still 'fiery and magnificent and tender'; none of them has anything to do with nationalist sentiment, or social and economic problems.

The 'Playboy' row

Synge always rejected any attempt at classification of *The Playboy*, and refused to disclose his own intentions in writing it. After the riots of the first production and a misleading published 'interview', however, he sent a letter to the *Irish Times* (which appeared on 31 January 1907) in which he declared: '*The Playboy of the Western World* is not a play with "a purpose" in the modern sense of the word, but although parts of it are, or are meant to be, extravagant comedy, still a great more that is behind it, is perfectly serious when looked at in a certain light. That is often the case, I think, with comedy, and no one is quite sure today whether "Shylock" and "Alceste" should be played seriously or not. There are, it may be hinted, several sides to *The Playboy*.'

The prolonged hostility which followed its first production suggests that the opponents of Synge's masterpiece were looking at it from *one* angle, though the angle was rarely the same. The first and most vociferous objections were made on moral and religious grounds. It was claimed that no village community would shelter, let alone welcome, a parricide; that no Irish girl would spend the night, unchaperoned, under the same roof as a young man; that revolt against parental authority would not be condoned in Ireland. Because of the frequent use of holy names and the variety of oaths and cursing, it was felt that a false image of Irish piety was being presented, all the more so as the author himself was a Protestant and therefore, so it was asserted, unqualified to portray the everyday life and language of Irish Catholics. Father Reilly, the local priest, was seen as narrow-minded and oppressive, which indeed he is. The gusto with which excessive drinking, cruelty to animals and law-breaking are described was seen as highly unflattering to the country as a whole. It was perhaps this aspect, combined with the extraordinary naïvety about the outside world, which irritated extreme nationalists most. They felt – with some justice – that independence would be less easily granted to a nation of drunkards, liars and fools. The duty of all good Irishmen was to present a picture of Ireland which, if not exactly the conventional 'land of saints and scholars', would at least be reassuring in its sobriety and good sense.

Synge's refusal to change his play (even Yeats and Lady Gregory, then his co-directors of the Abbey, urged some modification of the language) has been justified by posterity and by events. *The Playboy* is now recognised as a comic masterpiece and is regularly performed all over the world and in many foreign languages.

A note on the text

The first edition of the play was entitled *The Playboy of the Western World. A Comedy in Three Acts*. It was published in 1907 by Maunsel, Dublin, and subtitled *Volume X of the Abbey Theatre Series*. When it was reprinted in June 1909, it contained the preface by Synge. This early edition is based on notes found in various notebooks and files, a detailed list of which is provided in Appendix B, pp.293–4 of J.M. Synge, *Collected Works*, Volume IV, edited by Ann Saddlemyer, Oxford University Press, London, 1968. This text of the play is likely to remain the definitive one.

Other useful editions are listed in Part 5, including *The Playboy of the Western World and Riders to the Sea*, Unwin Paperbacks, London, 1979, which may be found useful for class work, and on which the page references in these Notes are based.

Part 2

Summaries
of THE PLAYBOY OF THE
WESTERN WORLD

A general summary

On the west coast of Ireland, in a country public-house, a young man, Christy Mahon, arrives from a distant county in the south-west. Visibly frightened of the police, and exhausted by his long journey, he yields to the questioning of the occupants of the public-house and confesses that he has killed his father with the blow of a loy, eleven days earlier. Instead of the condemnation and hostility one might expect, he wins the praise of the men for his courage and daring, and the admiration of the publican's daughter, Pegeen Mike. The latter, a pretty, intelligent girl of twenty, is engaged to Shawn Keogh, who is neither brave nor gallant, and who, moreover, seems completely under the thumb of the local priest, Father Reilly. Shawn is a second best, but in an area which has lost all its spirited young men, Pegeen's choice is very limited: 'Red Linahan, has a squint in his eye, and Patcheen is lame in his heel, or the mad Mulrannies were driven from California and they lost in their wits' (p.16). So for her the new arrival is a source of excitement and fresh hope. Christy finds himself the centre of attention and adulation: drinks are supplied, compliments fly round and, best of all, he is offered employment and the hospitality of the public-house, or shebeen. Later, an attractive young woman, the Widow Quin, who is a close neighbour, endeavours to carry him off to *her* house. His self-confidence and pleasure know no bounds.

Realising that the story of his 'murder' has made him a hero, he repeats it with poetic embellishments, each time winning praise and admiration from the villagers as he increases the weight of the blow and his own heroic role in the affair. Unfortunately his father arrives on the scene, with a bandaged head, it is true, but very much alive and determined to wreak vengeance on his son. Despite the efforts of the Widow Quin, who has probably seen through the Playboy (as he is now called) from the first, but is kindly enough to protect him, Old Mahon finally confronts his son (just after the latter has carried all before him at the local sports and has won 'the crowning prize', in the shape of Pegeen's consent to marry him), knocks him down and beats him publicly. Faced with the hostility of the crowd and Pegeen's bitter reproaches, Christy makes a desperate bid to recover his lost prestige and her affection by striking his father again and, apparently, killing him (off stage). But what was formerly a 'gallous story' or romantic tale, involving an unknown character in a distant place, has now become a dirty deed, involving someone they all know, under their very eyes. The villagers are preparing to hand him over to the police when Old Mahon returns yet again, this time on all fours, but still very much alive, expresses his contempt for the community and departs with his son. Now their roles are reversed; with Christy in charge, they appear to be reconciled at last. Life has returned to normal in this quiet parish for all save Pegeen, who ends the play with a bitter lament for the loss of the Playboy.

Detailed summaries

Act 1

In a remote depopulated district of the west of Ireland, inside a country public-house or shebeen, we meet Pegeen Mike, heroine of the play and daughter of the widowed publican, Michael James Flaherty. Pegeen, who is 'a wild-looking but fine girl of about twenty', is writing to the neighbouring town of Castlebar to order clothes and re-freshments for her wedding. While she is pretty, intelligent and high-spirited, her fiancé, Shawn Keogh, who soon arrives on the scene, is fat, stupid and cowardly. It quickly transpires that Pegeen's attitude to her fiancé is one of indifference, not to say contempt; and that her natural choice would be for a more courageous, more romantic young man, ready to defy the authorities, and less under the thumb of the local priest. But with most of the young men departed from the area, she apparently has to be content with Shawn, who is the 'approved' candi-date of her father and the priest.

We learn that Pegeen's father is about to set off for Kate Cassidy's wake, some distance off across the sands, with several of his cronies. (A wake is a watching over the body of a dead person, prior to burial. A strange survival of pre-Christian Ireland, it lasts all night, and is accompanied by heavy drinking and smoking, as well as pious reflections about the dead. It was a common occurrence in Ireland when Synge wrote his play, and still exists in many country parts.) Pegeen's fear of being left alone all night is heightened by Shawn's account of 'a fellow above in the furzy ditch, groaning wicked like a maddening dog' (p.17).

Michael James, who now returns to the shebeen with Philly Cullen and Jimmy Farrell, has also heard of the queer fellow in the ditch and, faced with Pegeen's reproaches at the prospect of being left alone, suggests that Shawn should keep her company while he and his friends attend the wake. However Shawn is too prudish to spend the night under the same roof as an unchaperoned girl, and anyhow is scared of Father Reilly's possible disapproval. 'I'm afeard of Father Reilly,' he says (p.19). Despite the efforts of the men to keep him there by force, he contrives to escape from the shebeen but, with characteristic cowardice, comes running back when he sees the 'queer dying fellow' approaching.

Christy Mahon, the hero of the play, now enters. In neat dramatic contrast to what we have been expecting, he is 'a slight young man, . . . very tired and frightened and dirty' and, apparently, on the run from the police. The arrival of any stranger in such a remote community is in itself an event; the fact that he has something to hide adds spice to his presence. Why is he afraid of the police? As audience, or readers, we share the curiosity of the characters in the public-house as they crowd round Christy and urge him to divulge his secret. The usual crimes are listed and dismissed: larceny, violence against unjust landlords, immorality, bigamy, forgery, and so on. Suspense and excitement increase as Christy rejects them all and suggests the greater gravity of his offence. Finally, after Pegeen has taunted him – 'You did nothing at all' (p.23) – and threatened him, the terrible truth emerges: he has killed his father.

Instead of hostility and disapproval, Christy finds himself the object of admiration and praise, partly no doubt because the victim is unknown to his listeners and the crime took place in 'a distant place . . . a windy corner of high, distant hills' (p.25) but also, perhaps, because any break in the dull routine of these isolated people is a welcome change in their lives. At all events, Christy's audience press him for further details, supply him with drinks and, to crown all, Pegeen and her father offer him employment and the hospitality of the shebeen. As the problem of leaving Pegeen alone has now been solved, Michael James and the others can leave for the wake with easy minds: 'with a man killed his father holding danger from the door' (p.26). Only Shawn Keogh, understandably disgruntled by the unexpected turn of events, is unwilling to leave Pegeen alone with a young man whose bravery is commended by all; but Pegeen, delighted with her new companion, dispatches poor Shawn unceremoniously: 'Go on, then, to Father Reilly and let him put you in the holy brotherhoods, and leave that lad to me' (p.27).

There follows the first of the three great scenes in the play when Pegeen and Christy are alone together. The latter has all the requisites of a romantic suitor, in Pegeen's eyes: delicate features, 'a kind of quality name', mysterious origins and the glamour of being a fugitive from justice; to which he is soon to add eloquence and poetic language. Encouraged by the compliments of the men and elated by the obvious admiration of this attractive young woman, Christy's joy knows no bounds. 'Expanding with delight at the first confidential talk he has ever had with a woman' – to quote the stage direction (p.29) – he finds within himself an inexhaustible well of eloquence and fine talk, to describe his nature, his background, his pursuits, his father. He changes and develops, acquiring self-confidence and beauty of speech before our very eyes.

Yet his boasting and self-esteem collapse when there is a knock at the door, and he clings to Pegeen like a frightened child. The visitor is the nearest neighbour, the Widow Quin, who comes, so she claims, with instructions from Father Reilly to take Christy to her own house. Older than Pegeen and wiser in the ways of the world, she probably sees through Christy from the start. Yet she is lonely enough to want a man for herself, and handsome enough to be a serious rival. The scene that follows is therefore rich in comedy, as the verbal battle between the two women briefly becomes a physical one, with Pegeen and the Widow Quin pulling at him from different sides. Summoned to decide, Christy says: 'It's here I'd liefer stay' (p.34) and thus opts for Pegeen, who has provided his supper and prepared his bed, and thanks to whose admiration and beauty he has found himself.

After the Widow Quin has left, defeated, and after Pegeen has bid him goodnight, he can hardly believe his good fortune: 'two fine women fighting for the likes of me – till I'm thinking this night wasn't I a foolish fellow not to kill my father in the years gone by' (p.35).

NOTES AND GLOSSARY:
Remembering that the play was written primarily for performance on the stage, notice that the first act fulfils its threefold dramatic function admirably: the scene is set; all the major characters (except Old Mahon) are introduced; excitement and curiosity are aroused. Furthermore, we are rapidly acquainted with the situation: Pegeen Mike is engaged to Shawn Keogh but would prefer a more romantic husband; Christy Mahon has killed his father in 'a distant place', and is therefore a fugitive from justice; Michael James Flaherty is off to the wake; the Widow Quin, like Pegeen herself, is interested in Christy. Thus everything that happens in this first act is designed to set the action in motion and create suspense about the future. Moreover the play unfolds in a precise area 'near a village, on a wild coast of Mayo', at a precise time (shortly after the Boer War), to a background of agrarian troubles and agitation against the British military presence in Ireland. The shebeen itself, where the three acts take place, is described in great detail, so that readers (as opposed to audience) may visualise the scene exactly. As the curtain falls on the first act, we are left asking a number of questions. When will retribution catch up with Christy?

How will the love affair between Pegeen and Christy develop? How will Shawn Keogh react to the presence of a rival at the shebeen? What will the Widow Quin do to be avenged on Pegeen, and further her own interests? When, and in what condition, will the 'wakers' return? In a word: what does the future hold?

creel cart: cart with wicker sides and back

Pegeen (without looking at him): as so often, the stage direction is eloquent. Normally, a young girl would look up at her fiancé

would I have a right: would it be my duty, should I . . .

scruff: back

peeler: policeman. Sir Robert Peel (1788–1854) instituted the Irish constabulary in the first half of the nineteenth century, and, later, reformed the police force in London

a great warrant to tell: a great fellow for telling

conceit: desire

furzy: overgrown with gorse

maddening: going mad

Is it a man you seen?: for this, and other peculiarities of 'Irish' English, see Part 3

let on: pretend

blabbing: gossiping

whisht: keep quiet, be silent

quitting off: going away

Stooks of the Dead Women: sharp rocks on the shore, pointed like stooks of corn

bad cess: bad luck

himself: here, the man of the house

afeard: afraid

in the gripe: in the hollow

noising: noise

minding: paying attention to

destroy: kill, injure, wear out

famished: dying

polis: police

a bona fide: a customer who has travelled three miles or more to reach the public-house and is thus entitled to drink alcohol after closing time

wanting: wanted by the police

strong farmer: prosperous farmer

the butt: the depths, end

puzzle-the-world: total mystery

fighting for the Boers: probably an allusion to a certain Arthur Lynch, who had fought against the British in South Africa. Synge knew him in Paris

so: in that case

Tuesday was a week: a week before last Tuesday

mister honey: origin unknown; an ingratiating form of address

crusty: bad-tempered

I've no licence, and I'm a law-fearing man: notice the unconscious irony

slaughter-boy: butcher

the way Jimmy Farrell hanged his dog from the licence: that is, to avoid paying the licence

I just riz the loy: I just raised the loy (a long, thin spade for cutting turf)

ridge: back

Christy (considering). Aye. I buried him then: this is Christy's first *lie* about the incident

spuds: potatoes

poteen: an illicit form of whisky, usually distilled from potatoes

foxy: cunning

pitchpike: pitch-fork

looséd khaki cut-throats: an unflattering allusion to the British soldiers in Ireland; compare 'thousand militia . . . walking idle through the land' (p.19)

droughty: thirsty

with a man killed his father holding danger from the door: notice the irony

the great powers and potentates of France and Spain: perhaps an allusion to the Patrick MacMahon (1808–98) of Irish origin who became President of France

limber: supple

streeleen: endless, eloquent talk

Owen Roe O'Sullivan: eighteenth-century poet from Kerry

a power: a great many

the like of a king of Norway or the eastern world: that is, with several wives

gaudy officer: refers to the brightly-coloured uniforms of the time

banbhs: young pigs

the divil a one: no one at all

seemly: handsome

stringing gabble: chattering endlessly

curiosity man: strange fellow

Shaneen:	little Shawn; 'een' is a diminutive form used in either affection or contempt
his likeness:	the like of him
overed it:	got over it, recovered
helter-skelter:	run wildly. Unusual as a verb
cuteness:	wisdom, shrewdness
abroad:	away from the house
sop:	wisp
grass tobacco:	dried but uncured tobacco
I'd liefer stay:	I'd prefer to stay
wary:	careful
blather:	idle talk
call:	need

Act 2

The next morning finds Christy in the same gay mood as the night before. As the curtain rises, we see him alone, cleaning Pegeen's boots and making a count of the bottles and glasses in the shebeen where, he believes, an easy life awaits him. No sooner does he start to wash his face and admire himself in a looking-glass, however, than he is interrupted by a bevy of village girls who have come to gaze on the man who killed his father.

In the following scene the girls gather round him admiringly, load him with gifts and flattery and, after the Widow Quin has joined the company, persuade him to retell his story, which he does willingly and with embellishments of every kind. In this new version his father has been 'split to the knob of his gullet' (p.41). Pegeen returns to find him drinking, arms linked with the Widow Quin, and soon dismisses the girls and puts him in his place by giving him a terrifying account of a hanging reported in the papers: 'a fearful end . . . and it worst of all for a man destroyed his da' (p.43). Young girls who go out with peelers, she adds pointedly, can hardly be counted on to keep the secret. Christy, frightened and cast down, prepares to take to the road again, but not before he has lyrically described his loneliness and his growing admiration for Pegeen; whereupon she relents and calls him back. His flirtatiousness with the girls forgiven – 'I wouldn't give a thraneen for a lad hadn't any spirit in him and a gamey heart' says Pegeen (p.46) – all seems set for a romantic scene, when Shawn Keogh arrives with the Widow Quin.

Having managed to get rid of Pegeen on a pretext of straying sheep, they proceed to try to discourage Christy from wooing her further. Shawn offers a ticket to America and a selection of fine clothes, stressing the unsuitability of such a match: 'and she with the divil's own temper' (p.47). Then, as Christy is trying on the clothes in the next room, he desperately promises the Widow Quin all sorts of rewards if only she will remove the danger. However Christy emerges, looking very smart in the new clothes, more arrogant than ever, and apparently determined to stay with Pegeen. Having motioned Shawn to leave, the Widow Quin is now alone with Christy, who, somewhat intoxicated by his success all round, refers again to the blow he dealt his father, this time 'to the breeches belt' (p.49). But just as he is about to sally forth, he sees Old Mahon approaching and recoils in terror. His *swaggering* quickly transformed into *staggering*, he once again appeals to a woman for protection.

There follows a scene of delightful comedy, heightened by suspense, as Christy, hiding behind the door, hears his father describe him to the Widow Quin in very unflattering terms: a lazy good-for-nothing ('a lier on walls'), useless on the farm and scared of the girls ('If he seen a red petticoat coming swinging over the hill, he'd be off to hide in the sticks', p.51), and unable to drink or smoke without ill effects. The boaster is brought low as the entranced Widow Quin leads Old Mahon on; but in the end she protects Christy from his father's vengeance by misdirecting the latter across the sands to chastise his errant son. Now mistress of the situation, she listens aghast while Christy curses his father with astonishing eloquence (p.53); makes an attempt to win him for herself and disillusion him about Pegeen; and finally, moved by the obvious intensity of his feelings, promises her assistance and connivance in exchange for much the same advantages as Shawn had promised 'the time that you'll be master here' (p.54).

The act ends rather ironically with Christy hailed off to the sports by the admiring village girls, while the Widow Quin, with characteristic realism and good humour, predicts the future.

NOTES AND GLOSSARY:
Act 2 answers most of the questions posed by Act 1 and introduces us to the last important character, Old Mahon. We watch the see-saw of Christy's fortunes: delighted and encouraged by the admiration of the girls, he is quickly subdued by Pegeen Mike; swelling with pride at Shawn's attempts to buy him off, and 'mighty spruce' in the borrowed garments, he is humiliated and enraged by his father's cruel portrait. Yet through it all he is growing in self-confidence, in self-assurance and in the power of speech.

Dramatically, the arrival of Old Mahon adds a new dimension to the play, increasing our excitement and suspense. How long will his presence in the area be known only to Christy and the Widow Quin? When will the encounter between father and son take place; and how will the villagers, and in particular Pegeen, react to it?

Psychologically, Shawn and the Widow Quin have developed, the former revealing his unscrupulous, cowardly nature: 'If I wasn't so God-fearing, I'd near have courage to come behind him and run a pike into his side' (p.48); the latter showing her ingenuity, humour and common sense, with a dash of romance thrown in: 'thinking on the gallant hairy fellows are drifting beyond' (p.53).

beyond:	over there
to drunken:	make drunk
in it:	there
Belmullet:	the nearest town
cnuceen:	little hill
nursing a feast:	holding the food in his arms
gamey:	merry
treacherous:	apparently used as a compliment!
dray:	farm cart, or truck
scythe . . . loy:	notice how the story is growing
outlandish:	foreign
parching peelers . . . English law:	this speech gave offence to the English authorities in Dublin
jobbing:	employed from time to time
penn'orth:	pennyworth
frish-frash:	dregs
shut of jeopardy:	out of danger
swiggling:	maybe a blend of 'swing' and 'wriggle'
Neifin, Erris:	local places
walking:	living
hard set:	at a loss
scalded:	tormented
wattle:	stick
mitch:	play truant
leaguing:	joining
a thraneen:	the least scrap, something of no value
cleeve:	basket
get shut of me:	get rid of me
loan:	lend
Kilmainham:	a well-known gaol in Dublin
pike:	pitch-fork
contrivance:	device, scheme
turbary:	the right to cut turf
Crossmolina, Ballina:	towns in County Mayo
the western world:	here, the United States
tramper:	tramp
streeler:	idler

gob:	mouth
felts:	small birds
making mugs . . .:	compare with the incident of the looking-glass earlier in the act
the spit of you:	just like you. Note the poetic justice with which Old Mahon is punished for his lack of paternal feelings
pull up on:	catch up with
civil warrior:	decent man
playboy:	tricky, unreliable, boastful person
spavindy:	lame with spavin, a disease of the hock joint
shift:	a woman's undergarment reaching to the knees
hookers:	fishing-boats
curagh:	a light narrow boat, made of laths covered with tarred canvas

Act 3

Jimmy and Philly return from the wake, slightly drunk. They have heard of Christy's successes at the fair and sports, and fall to wondering whether his persistent bragging may not lead to his arrest, and speculating on what has happened to Old Mahon's body: 'A man can't hang by his own informing, and his father should be rotten by now' says Jimmy (p.56). Old Mahon then returns again incognito, and is giving his version of what happened when the Widow Quin enters. With typical resourcefulness, she calms him down with a glass of poteen and tries to persuade the others that he is a wandering maniac, totally unconnected with Christy. Meanwhile Old Mahon, growing loquacious under the influence of the drink, resumes the story of Christy as a good-for-nothing son, and his portrait is so different from the daring, athletic playboy the villagers have learnt to admire that the Widow Quin is able for the time being to allay the suspicions of the others, who are troubled by the coincidences involved.

As the chief event of the sports begins, all four mount on the bench to watch through the window; and the excitement of the mule race, with Christy's victory, is conveyed to the audience (or readers) through the vivid comments of the watchers. But Old Mahon has recognised his son: 'I'd know his way of spitting and he astride the moon' (p.61), and it requires all the Widow Quin's skill to persuade him that he is only suffering from a return of madness: 'Oh, I'm raving with a madness that would fright the world,' he confesses (p.61). Resigned to his state, and even proud of it, he prepares to leave for the asylum to avoid the persecution of a pitiless community 'for them lads caught a maniac one time and pelted the poor creature,' says the Widow Quin (p.62). Only Philly suspects something fishy in the whole proceeding and resolves to investigate further.

Old Mahon's departure is rapidly succeeded by Christy's triumphant return, flushed with success, and the hero of the day. When the crowd leaves to watch the last event, the Playboy is now alone with Pegeen for the third time. Emboldened by his series of triumphs and by her obvious admiration for him, Christy declares his love in flights of lyrical prose (pp.64, 65). Their love scene is however cut short by the drunken return of Michael James, supported by Shawn. Maybe Christy is thinking uneasily of his own father's excesses, as he listens to the publican's inebriated speeches.

. Matters are quickly brought to a head when Michael James announces the arrival of the 'dispensation' and Pegeen declares that she intends to marry Christy. Appalled at first by the prospect, her father tries to make Shawn jealous; but the latter's cowardice is stronger than any feeling he may have for Pegeen: 'I'd be afeard to be jealous of a man did slay his da,' he says (p.68). Disgusted by this 'quaking blackguard', Michael James agrees to bless the union of Pegeen and the Playboy; but their hopes are dashed by the third entry of Old Mahon (now accompanied by the crowd), who knocks Christy down and starts beating him in front of all. Christy's feeble attempts to deny the relationship convince no one; and the disillusionment of the villagers is echoed more strongly by Pegeen's bitter repudiation of her hero: 'And to think of the coaxing glory we had given him, and he after doing nothing but hitting a soft blow and chasing northward in a sweat of fear. Quit off from this' (p.70). The last words are a word-for-word repetition of Christy's dismissal of the cowardly Shawn (p.69). Thus, in a dramatic reversal of fortune, Christy finds himself surrounded by enemies calling for retribution on him. In a desperate attempt to regain his lost prestige and Pegeen's love, he picks up the loy in the shebeen, chases Old Mahon out and, apparently, really kills him this time. But the shadowy figure in his tale is very different from the flesh-and-blood visitor to Mayo, and his hopes – 'I'm thinking, from this out, Pegeen'll be giving me praises, the same as in the hours gone by' (p.73) – are ill-founded. For, as Pegeen remarks, 'there's a great gap between a gallous story and a dirty deed' (p.74). The village people have turned against him and the Widow Quin's attempts to smuggle him away disguised as a woman are unavailing. The villagers throw a rope over his head and prepare to hand him over to the police.

In the following scene the play approaches farce, as Christy bites Shawn's leg, after threatening all and sundry with terrible vengeance and giving a sentimental account of his own imagined end; as Pegeen scorches Christy's leg to make him let go the table; and finally as Old Mahon makes his last entry on all fours. The latter's contempt for 'the villainy of Mayo, and the fools is here' (p.77) leads to a reconciliation with his newly-respected son, who has become 'master of all fights from now' (p.77). In an ending which has always been a subject of controversy, Christy expresses his gratitude to the community: 'for you've turned me a likely gaffer in the end of all' (p.73); Michael James welcomes a return to the normal: 'By the will of God, we'll have peace now for our drinks' (p.77); and Shawn's hopes of marriage with Pegeen are restored. Only Pegeen is inconsolable, as the curtain falls, in lamenting her loss: 'I've lost the only Playboy of the Western World' (p.77).

NOTES AND GLOSSARY:
Act 3 is the richest of the acts, both in dramatic content and in colourful language. Once we know that Old Mahon has not left the area we are ready for anything; and his *three* returns in the course of the act are fraught with excitement. Meanwhile the love affair between Pegeen and Christy is progressing fast, and Shawn, true to himself, is earning the contempt of all. As for the language, it reaches new heights of eloquence and poetry throughout, whether we consider the comic interlude with Jimmy and Philly, Old Mahon's account of his mad fits, Michael James's 'nuptial' speech or the rising lyricism of Christy and Pegeen as they 'imagine' their love together.

gaffer: young fellow, lad
roulette man . . . cockshot man: attractions at the fair
lepping: jumping
Old Mahon passes window slowly: notice how the suspense is sustained
hobbled: fettered, put in gaol
Dublin: in the National Museum there
winning clean beds and the fill of my belly: notice that Christy has been similarly rewarded for *his* version of the 'story'
supeen: a drop of drink.
unravelling: explaining
next and nighest: a typical tautology for nearest of kin
skelping: beating
brain-pan: head
winkered: with blinkers on
dilly-dallying: delaying
hap'orth: halfpennyworth
more power to the young lad!: may strength be with him!
hooshing: hoisting, encouraging
abetting: encouraging
lug: ear

likely:	promising
parlatic:	paralytic
union:	workhouse, where paupers were fed and housed in return for a little labour
astray:	demented, wandering
gaming:	deceit, trickery
darlint:	darling
blackthorn:	a stick made from the blackthorn tree
a while since:	a while ago
when Good Friday's by:	that is after Lent, the period of abstinence for good Catholics
such poet's talking, and such bravery of heart:	notice the association of the two qualities
Owen, Carrowmore:	local rivers
paters:	paternosters, that is, recitals of the Lord's Prayer
jackstraw:	least straw
till I'd marry a Jew-man, with ten kegs of gold:	Pegeen, too, has romantic fancies. Compare the Widow Quin's speech on p.53
townland:	district
stretched out retching speechless on the holy stones:	one of the phrases that gave offence at the time ('retch' means 'vomit')
louty:	like a lout, loutish
unbeknownst:	secretly
smart:	strong
gilded:	perhaps because of the lettering, or the cost
gallous:	corruption of 'gallows'; here, 'fine'
crusted:	encrusted
middling kind of a scarecrow:	a poor specimen
drownded:	drowned
when it's sooner on a bullock's liver . . .:	notice the neat contrast implied between Shawn and Christy
drift of heifers:	herd of heifers
Sneem:	a village in Kerry
Take the loy is on your western side:	in country places, points of a compass are often used for very short distances
quit off:	depart
fine weather be after him:	good riddance
renege:	go back on a promise
gallant swearers . . . puny weeds:	again the implied contrast between the two suitors
quenched:	killed
slitted:	with his throat cut

scorch of haste:	burning hurry
Munster:	the southern province of Ireland
slate:	punish
the old hen:	influenza
cholera morbus:	a dangerous, infectious disease
Keel:	in Achill, County Mayo
pandied:	beaten like a schoolboy

You're after making a mighty man of me this day by the power of a lie: these words might be said to sum up the play's theme

winking:	blinking with astonishment

raise the top-knot on a poet in a merchant's town: bring praise for eloquence, even in uncultivated surroundings

again:	local form of against

What good'd be my lifetime if I left Pegeen?: but he does! Notice the irony

a drift of chosen females, standing in their shifts itself: another phrase that gave offence

Let you take it Pegeen: Shawn Keogh excels himself in cowardice here

stretch:	lay out dead
a great gap:	that is, Old Mahon is no longer fictitious

would liefest wreak his pains on me: would prefer to choose me as the object of his violence

a gallous jaunt:	a wonderful journey
Limbo:	region in the confines of hell

Ladies in their silks and satins . . . fate?: a blend of self-pity and romantic fancy

He's the like of a mad dog: compare with Shawn's first description of Christy (p.17)

It is the will of God . . . itself?: notice how Michael James voices the sentiment of the villagers when faced with *real* murder (as they believe)

Part 3

Commentary

The making of the play: dramatic craftsmanship

Of Synge's six major plays (see Part 5), *The Playboy of the Western World* is the one which underwent most careful revision and most experimental handling. A glance at the worksheets and commentary in Appendix B of J.M. Synge, *Collected works, Volume IV* will show how many 'plots' and titles were considered and rejected; how many characters and incidents were introduced, modified or enlarged. Between the first rough draft (made late in 1904), in which the play opens with a fight in the potato garden between Old Mahon (at this stage called O'Flaherty) and his son, and the version which was finally performed in January 1907, many schemes were thought out and listed, including one in four acts. Yet once Synge believed the play was ready for the stage, he refused to change one iota of it. He was, said Lady Gregory in a letter to Yeats, 'like a tiger with its cub'. We may therefore reasonably assume that the final version was the fruit of long reflection and immense care, an unalterable work of art. What then were Synge's qualifications as a playwright?

He had read widely in Elizabethan and Jacobean drama. He had seen many of Molière's (1622–73) comedies on the stage in Paris (and read all his works, in 1896). Above all, in five annual visits to the Aran Islands (see Part 1), he had found the source of four of his plays and, as he says himself, 'learned to write the peasant dialect and dialogue which I use in my plays'. He thus came to play writing with strong qualifications and a solid groundwork; and a deep awareness, most of all, of the need for visual effects on the stage. Let us consider *The Playboy* from the point of view of dramatic craftsmanship.

Stage directions

What strikes the reader of the play first is the number of stage directions. (The spectator in the theatre is only aware of these indirectly, that is, in so far as the producer makes effective use of them.) Synge is meticulous about dress and furniture: the colour and texture of the first, the exact position of the second. His description of the shebeen is a model of precision, based on close observation during his travels round Ireland. As each character appears, a few words serve to suggest his appearance and character. Expressions, gestures, movements and moods are portrayed with swift strokes of the pen, so much so that we sometimes wonder whether the directions are not overdone, leaving the potential producer with inadequate room for manoeuvre in interpreting the play. Yet these indications are precious at key moments, as for instance when Christy, pressed for details about the disposal of his avowedly murdered father says '[*considering*]: Aye. I buried him then' and thus, in telling his first lie, prepares us for future embellishments of the tale; or later, when overcome by the flattery of the girls and the attempted bribery of Shawn Keogh, he *swaggers* to the door, tightening his belt, only to *stagger* back at the sight of his murdered da. Here, as elsewhere, everything is *seen* by Synge. One thinks of the drunken movements of Jimmy and Philly in Act 3, the arrival of Old Mahon, the dismay of the Widow Quin, and the way in which the excitement of the mule race is conveyed by the gestures and reactions of the watchers through the window.

Nothing is left to chance. From the last romantic scene between Pegeen and Christy to the drunken return of Michael James, every movement is prepared, every tone of voice suggested. Right to the end, Synge is instructing the characters exactly how to gesticulate, speak, react. Having watched the plays of Molière in Paris and the Abbey players in Dublin, he knew exactly what he wanted and what could be done on the stage to obtain it. Most of all, his chief creation, Christy Mahon, is revealed to us in a series of changing moods and postures: doleful, bashful and timid at the outset; flattered and swelling with triumph as he gains confidence; delighted, enraptured and eloquent as he wins Pegeen's affection; arrogant, proud and swaggering as he comes to dominate the community; threatening and self-confident at the end. It is a very testing role for an actor; but the dramatist is always there directing, advising, encouraging, and saying precisely how the lines should be spoken to achieve maximum effect.

Exits and entrances

Hand in hand with such detailed stage direction goes a masterly skill in the management of exits and entrances. These are used variously: to point a contrast, as when Christy, who has been described by Shawn as 'groaning wicked like a maddening dog' (p.17) and by Michael James as 'a queer fellow above, going mad' (p.19), enters 'very tired and frightened and dirty' (p.21), or when Old Mahon and Christy make their final exit with the father/son relationship reversed; to sustain suspense and excitement, as when Pegeen returns from the hill to find 'her' Christy the centre of female admiration, 'leaguing with the girls' (p.41), and especially when Old Mahon returns from the 'dead' which he does no less than four times (a *tour de force* this, a feat of skill un-equalled in modern drama); to debunk vanity, boasting and lies, as happens on three of Old Mahon's returns, or when Christy clings to Pegeen in terror when someone knocks, just after he has been vaunting himself as 'a seemly fellow with great strength in me and bravery' (p.31).

Visual comedy

Richest of all, perhaps, are the scenes of pure visual comedy. The spectator is alternately tickled and delighted by Shawn escaping the clutches of Michael James and leaving his coat in the latter's hands (p.20); by the sight of the Widow Quin and Pegeen tugging at Christy from different sides (a neat reversal of the old convention, with the man being pursued) (p.33); by Christy trying to conceal the looking-glass from the village girls (p.38); by Jimmy and Philly's drunken dialogue with Old Mahon in Act 3; by Old Mahon's last entrance on hands and knees, 'coming to be killed a third time' (p.76).

If other scenes seem excessively farcical – Michael James singing drunkenly, Christy biting Shawn's leg, Pegeen scorching Christy's – it should be remembered that the title of Synge's first draft was 'The Murderer, a farce' and that the hero himself is involved in most of such scenes. In this way the romantic aspect is nicely counterpointed by a frankly Rabelaisian note (that is, suggesting robust low comedy and caricature), as for instance when Christy's flights of poetic eloquence in the last and greatest love scene are interrupted by drunken singing, and the lovers return to everyday life with a shock of disillusionment.

Use of contrast

The use of contrast – one of the oldest devices in comedy – is exploited at many levels. Physical contrast at first: with fat Shawn and slight Christy; fat Jimmy and thin Philly; jovial Michael James and cranky Old Mahon; twenty-year-old Pegeen and thirty-year-old Widow Quin. More subtly, the contrast in character: between the wild, passionate, romantic Pegeen and the calm, detached, matter-of-fact widow; between the conventional, pious, cowardly Shawn and the imaginative, adventurous, brave Christy; between Michael James, the symbol of paternal authority ('I never cursed my father' says Pegeen) (p.31), rooted in Mayo, and Old Mahon, whose authority has been flouted, and who is uprooted from his native Kerry.

Yet all these contrasts, physical, moral and situational, are emphasised by similarities. Pegeen and the Widow Quin are both poetic in speech and adept at verbal duelling, both anxious to win Christy; Shawn and the Playboy are both orphaned and both seeking marriage, both anxious to win Pegeen; Michael James and Old Mahon are both widowed, both concerned with one child for whom they have chosen a 'suitable' spouse, both hard drinkers. Behind all the characters is the implicit clash between the wandering Mahons and the settled Mayo community, brought home to us at the end by the spokesmen of the conflicting ideologies when Christy says 'I'll go romancing through a romping lifetime' and Michael James rejoins 'By the will of God, we'll have peace now for our drinks.'

Absent characters

One of the most striking features of Synge's dramatic craftsmanship is the part played by absent characters. Chief of these in *The Playboy* is Father Reilly, who is with us in spirit from the beginning till the end of the play. Mentioned some dozen times, he is a character entirely created through the words of others, representing the ever-present, ever-watchful Catholic Church in the rural Ireland of seventy-five years ago. Respectable, pious and orthodox, he enshrines the deeply-embedded doctrines and values of the Irish Catholic peasant. To Shawn Keogh, the priest is a rock of certainty, incarnating 'the peace we had till last night at the fall of dark' (p.47), before the Playboy's bohemian intrusion. The degree to which his authority is recognised by Shawn and questioned by Pegeen, the extent to which we feel his presence (he is never very far off-stage, we think) are the best proof of Synge's achievement in creating a living character whom we never see. Other living characters whom we know only indirectly are the Widow Casey (another widow), whom Old Mahon has chosen to be his son's wife: 'A walking terror from beyond the hills . . . and she a woman of noted misbehaviour with the old and young' (p.40); and Marcus Quin: 'God rest him, got six months for maiming ewes, and he a great warrant to tell stories of Holy Ireland' (p.17). Related to these 'absent' characters are the portraits of Old Mahon and Christy as each one sees the other in distant Kerry: the crusty, bibulous father 'rising up in the red dawn . . . and shying clods against the visage of the stars' (p.30); the good-for-nothing son 'a dirty, stuttering lout . . . a lier on walls, a talker of folly' (p.50).

The Playboy has frequently been commended for its poetic language and for its roaring comedy. It has been praised or shouted down as a picture of Irish life. What has received insufficient attention is its outstanding dramatic skill. When Synge came to write this comedy, his craftsmanship had reached something close to perfection. In its consummate blending of romance and farce, it recalls Shakespeare's mature comedies, allowing of course for a different context and a different age. While full appreciation of the stagecraft can come only when the play is seen in the theatre, a great deal can be learned from a study of the means employed.

Characters

Christy Mahon

Christy is the character who develops most in the course of the play. The stage directions in Act 1 show how frightened, timid and bashful he is on arrival at the public-house. Gradually, as he is induced to tell his story and finds that the reaction to his 'deed' is favourable, he acquires self-confidence and the power of poetic language. In the eyes of the men he is 'a daring fellow' and (potentially) 'a great terror when his temper's roused' (p.25), while Pegeen's solicitude and admiration, her subsequent praise of his looks and personality, fill him with growing pride. By the end of Act 1, after the Widow Quin's flattering attempts to carry him off, and Pegeen's kindly ministrations, he has become extraordinarily sure of himself. We are thus prepared for the successes that follow in Act 2: with the village girls, with Pegeen (after a temporary setback), with Shawn Keogh. Even Old Mahon's 'resurrection' deflates him only temporarily; and he leaves for the sports with an admiring female escort. After his athletic victories and Pegeen's promise to marry him, we see him brought low by an enraged father, repudiated by the villagers and rejected by Pegeen. Yet these reverses are seemingly as nothing at the end, when, transformed, he declares himself 'master of all fights from now' (p.77) and, grown up at last, he leaves in quest of fresh adventures, with his father subdued and Pegeen apparently forgotten. How has this transformation taken place and to what extent is it plausible?

Our picture of Christy is filled in bit by bit, throughout the first two acts: by his own self-descriptions to Pegeen; by the vivid flashbacks (returns to past incidents) provided by Old Mahon; by stray comments from the other characters. From all this, and from his own words, we learn that he has been a day-dreamer, shy of the girls yet conscious of his own appearance, ill-fitted for farm work and for the drinking and smoking that is, apparently, the best proof of virility in his home context. Are we to conclude that there has always been a hero and a poet beneath the surface; and that the Mayo community and Pegeen provide the conditions for the emergence of this dominating character? An original, arresting, complex character, he remains something of a mystery, a series of contradictions: alternately shy and aggressive, bashful and boastful, frightened and furious. From his first diffident entry to his last triumphant exit, he holds our attention. He is never dull. Is he convincing? In the letter quoted on p.13 (of the text), Synge suggests his subtlety; elsewhere the dramatist compares him with Shakespeare's Shylock and Molière's Alceste, neither of whom is a purely comic creation. The force of the opposition to him at the end of the play is a measure of the jealousy he has aroused, and of the strength of his personality. If his love for Pegeen seemed genuine, by the end he has gone far beyond this, and she appears as just a step in his ladder to success and adventure. Any study of his character must end with a series of questions. Will he be able to forget Pegeen for long? Will he not wish to return to the scene of his first triumphs in love and sport? Will he manage to maintain the new relationship with his father – 'a gallant captain with his heathen slave' (p.77)? These questions are outside the scope of the play; yet we feel the dramatist would like each spectator (or reader) to attempt an answer.

Pegeen Mike

Young, attractive and intelligent, Pegeen is a fine creation, a fascinating blend of contradictory characteristics. Despite her romantic, imaginative nature, she has agreed to a marriage without love, for reasons of convention and financial interest. Her 'intended', Shawn Keogh, is lumpish, unenterprising and cowardly, a slave to the Church and its precepts; but there is no one else available, so she has become engaged, with the twofold blessing of her father and the priest. After all, Shawn has land and cattle, a certain social position; and he is unlikely to prove unfaithful. Throughout the play, we have glimpses of this conventional, practical side of Pegeen. Her admiration for Christy's revolt against paternal authority is balanced by respect for her own father: 'I never killed my father. I'd be afeared to do that' (p.29); 'I never cursed my father the like of that, though I'm twenty and more years of age' (p.31). Her adulation of the Playboy, 'a fine lad with the great savagery to destroy your da' (p.45), 'fit to be holding his head high with the wonders of the world' (p.32), should be set against her sharp treatment of him after his 'leaguing with the girls' in Act 2, and against her immediate rejection when she sees his story is groundless in Act 3. Nevertheless she is highly romantic, idealising Christy from the start, as aristocratic in origin, one of the company of poets, 'fine, fiery fellows with great rages when their temper's roused' (p.28), and a great success with the girls. Earlier, she has idealised the men of action: 'the like of Daneen Sullivan knocked the eye from a peeler; or Marcus Quin, God rest him, got six months for maiming ewes' (p.17).

In her final love scene with Christy, when she shows herself his equal in poetic language, she describes herself revealingly: 'a girl was tempted often to go sailing the seas till I'd marry a Jew-man, with ten kegs of gold' (p.65). But the flights of fine talk and tenderness must be compared with her occasional sharpness of tongue – 'And to think it's me is talking sweetly, Christy Mahon, and I the fright of seven townlands for my biting tongue' – as we see in her exchanges with Shawn Keogh and the Widow Quin, especially, but indeed throughout the play, whenever she is crossed. Anxious to escape the dreary environment of the shebeen and the stultifying influence of a remote, depopulated, country region, she responds ardently to Christy's advances, revealing in the scenes with him great depths of sweetness and love, only to suffer cruel disillusionment at the end, when her house of dreams comes crashing down, and once again she faces the prospect of life with Shawn Keogh. Despite the box on the ear she gives the latter, we feel sure that she will compromise in marriage after all, with Father Reilly's blessing. If for Christy the future is one of 'romancing through a romping lifetime', for her it can only be tragic and gloomy, the reverse of the conventional happy ending.

Widow Quin

The Widow Quin is the perfect foil to Pegeen Mike in age, experience and character. As a thirty-year-old widow who has 'buried her children and destroyed her man' (p.55), she harbours few illusions about the world or its inhabitants. She judges Christy accurately from the first – 'and you fitter to be saying your catechism than slaying your da' (p.32); withstands Pegeen's bitter attacks with calm and good humour (p.33); and warns the Playboy what he may expect from a life with Pegeen. She is often an *anti-romantic* in her descriptions of the latter: 'who'd go helter-skeltering after any man would let you a wink upon the road' (p.33); 'a girl you'd see itching and scratching, and she with a stale stink of poteen on her from selling in the shop' (p.53); 'isn't there the match of her in every parish public?' (p.73). She is still, however, capable of romantic flights herself, as when she tells Christy of her lonely life and wistful fancies (pp.53, 54). We remember her too for her kindness to Christy (her attitude is more maternal and protective than Pegeen's) whom she tries to save right to the end, using one device after another; and for her acute business sense in bargaining successively with Shawn Keogh and the Playboy in Act 2. Finally she is gay, sociable and good-humoured; and wonderfully adaptable to people and events.

The Widow Quin is a key-figure in the play. Transformed from being merely one of the village girls (in an early draft) to her special rank as a widow of experience, she becomes in her creator's hands a central figure, in danger of overshadowing Pegeen at times, with her wit, vivacity, resourcefulness and calm contemplation of the human comedy. Her authority over the younger women, her refusal to be over-awed by Pegeen (on Pegeen's sudden arrival in Act 2, she remains seated while the others spring away from Christy in confusion), her energy and wisdom, mark her out as an exceptional character. A shrewd judge of people (she is never really taken in by the Playboy), she manages to win the confidence of both Shawn and Christy. It is she who enters the latter for the sports where he wins such fame; she who prepares, directs and supervises Shawn's attempts to get rid of his rival in Act 2; she who first of the Mayo community sees Old Mahon and keeps him at bay. In this way, she holds the strings of the action in her hands, and at the end of Act 2 she seems to be sitting pretty whatever happens: 'Well, if the worst comes in the end of all, it'll be great game to see there's none to pity him but a widow woman, the like of me' (p.55). It is no fault of hers when Old Mahon returns; and despite her inventive skill, her ingenuity is overtaxed at the end, as she admits when she says in reply to Christy's appeal: 'I've tried a lot, God help me, and my share is done' (p.71). In making one last effort to spirit him away, disguised as a girl, she is guilty of her only serious error of judgement: she underestimates the strength of Christy's love for Pegeen.

Finally, apart from her vital role in directing so much of the action, she is used as a kind of chorus, commenting on youth: 'Well, it's a terror to be aged a score' (p.34), on love, on life, with perception and good sense (though often cynically); and informing us of the situation as it evolves. She is both a living person and a necessary part of the plot.

Shawn Keogh

Shawn is a more conventional character than any of the others. Stupid, cowardly and slow, he belongs to traditional comedy. In all the situations which affect him, he refers explicitly, or implicitly, to Father Reilly, whose views on marriage, propriety and morality generally are his only touchstone. Any feeling of sympathy we might have for him fades when we are faced with his lack of intelligence and his total subservience to the Church. Unable to understand Pegeen's longing for a more exciting life, a more open society, he is terrified and overcome by the Playboy's arrival. All he wants is a return to 'the peace we had till last night at the fall of dark (p.47). His fear of Father Reilly, and his outrageous cowardice, fill us at the best with amusement, at the worst with contempt. When he leaves his coat in Michael James's hands; when he appeals to the Widow Quin to help him get rid of Christy; when he refuses to fight for the honour of his bride-to-be; when, at the end, he joins the others, from a safe distance, in overmastering the Playboy, we can only despise him. Yet, if he is a thoroughly despicable character, he provides many of the most comic moments in the play. When Pegeen taxes him with his lack of romance – 'when it's sooner on a bullock's liver you'd put a poor girl thinking than on the lily or the rose' – he can only reply: 'And have you no mind of my weight of passion, and the holy dispensation, and the drift of heifers I'm giving, and the golden ring?' (p.68). A curious mixture of factors!

Michael James

Like his cronies, Philly and Jimmy, Michael James is prominent at the beginning and in the third act. When we meet him in Act 1, he is preparing to go to the wake and brushing aside Pegeen's objections to being left alone all night. He is certainly fond of his daughter; but nothing will stop him from going to the wake where good company and 'flows of drink' await him. Every time we see him he is drinking or drunk, or talking about drink. He seems to have a poor opinion of his future son-in-law: 'by the will of God I've got you a decent man, Pegeen' (p.20) he says ironically, after Shawn has fled the prospect of spending the night under the same roof as his fiancée. Later he leads the questioning of Christy and treats him with kindness and hospitality, finally offering him the job of pot-boy. His attitude to the peelers, 'decent, droughty poor fellows', his pride in his establishment, his easy-going way of life, help to complete the portrait of a typical country publican of the time.

In the third act, however, when he returns drunk from the wake with his tongue loosened, we see a rather different person: loquacious, aggressive and exalting marriage and virility. His speech of 'blessing' over Pegeen and Christy shows him an enemy to celibacy, just as his earlier words showed him a foe to abstinence. He has an almost pagan joy in the rites of sex and drink. Yet he, too, turns against the Playboy at the end, remembering his responsibilities as a law-abiding father, whose duty it is to protect his daughter and ensure her material welfare.

Old Mahon

Christy's father is a character built on the heroic scale. He is first presented to us indirectly through his son's vivid description of his crusty nature, his wild drinking bouts and his eccentric behaviour. We learn of his large family, scattered over the world: 'and not a one of them, to this day, but would say their seven curses on him' (p.30); of his bad language and the insulting terms used to his own son: 'you squinting idiot', and so on. So we are not disappointed when he appears to the Widow Quin in Act 2, for his manners are gruff, his language violent and his intentions clearly bloodthirsty. His account of Christy's character and behaviour, so different from the image the latter has been projecting of himself (with help from the whole community), is colourful and rich in comic undertones. There is clearly a great discrepancy between one of the 'wonders of the western world' (p.41) and the 'looney of Mahon's' (p.51); between 'a fine, handsome young fellow with a noble brow' (p.28) and 'a small, low fellow . . . dark and dirty' (p.51).

In Act 3 he comes into his own, telling us the 'dunce never reached his second book' (p.58); of his own terrible fits of madness: 'There was one time I seen ten scarlet divils letting on they'd cork my spirit in a gallon can' (p.62); of his drunken exploits 'drinking myself silly and parlatic from the dusk to dawn' (p.62); exalting his wild state to a kind of grandeur 'with seven doctors writing out my sayings in a printed book' (p.62); beating his son publicly and reducing the latter's heroic deed to the cowardly blow of an 'ugly liar'. Even the second blow of a loy does not subdue him for long, or prevent him from making a biting judgement of the community, that was first foolish enough to believe the Playboy's story and then that the father could be so easily 'quenched': 'my son and myself will be going our own way, and we'll have great times from this out telling stories of the villainy of Mayo, and the fools is here' (pp.76, 77). It seems unlikely that Old Mahon, who has survived two ferocious blows on the head, the trials of a long journey on foot, and the consequences of excessive drinking, will easily allow his son to get the upper hand; however amused he may appear at the transformation of the 'dirty, stuttering lout', or at the reversal of the father/son roles.

Philly and Jimmy

The publican's friends form a traditional comic pair, the one, thin and mistrusting, the other, fat and amorous. Even looking at them arouses laughter the way characters such as the American film actors Laurel and Hardy do in the cinema. Indeed their chief function appears to be the provision of visual comedy, though they join Michael James in teasing Shawn Keogh and questioning Christy in Act 1, forming a kind of comic chorus, as the latter rejects one explanation after another of his fear of the police (p.23). Like Michael James, they are anxious to be off to the wake and, like him, they return from it drunk, the next day. It is this drunken return that provides them with their best scene, part comic irrelevance and part dramatic underscoring, as they talk of skulls and bones and the strange consequences of madness. Later they are used to convey the excitement of the mule race and of Christy's victory. They never appear separately, or reveal themselves more than superficially; but they add greatly to our enjoyment of the play.

The village girls

Here, too, the function is chiefly to enhance other characters and please the eye. The four attractive girls are used to boost Christy's pride and increase his self-confidence, which they do by gathering round him flirtatiously, loading him with gifts and, especially, praising his tale:

> SUSAN: That's a grand story.
> HONOR: He tells it lovely. (p.41)

They also provide visual comedy as they compel Christy to reveal the mirror he is holding behind his back, or as Sara puts on his boots. A further dramatic function is the way they comment on the social background. Susan stresses the uneventfulness of local life when she accuses Sara of being 'the one yoked the ass cart and drove ten miles to set your eyes on the man bit the yellow lady's nostril on the northern shore' (p.37); and the latter echoes her sadly, saying 'you'd be ashamed this place, going up winter and summer with nothing worth while to confess at all' (p.37). Sara makes another brief appearance towards the end when she offers her petticoat to disguise the Playboy; but there is no attempt to develop her, or the others, psychologically.

Language and style

Synge's language has always been a source of difficulty for those who are not familiar with the kind of English that is spoken in Ireland. The chief reason for this difference is that while English had been spoken in Ireland for centuries, Irish remained the first language of the people, in country parts at least, till well into the eighteenth century. As a result, the English that was acquired by Irish people showed, and still shows, the influence of the native Irish language: in syntax, in vocabulary, in pronunciation.

In *The Playboy of the Western World*, this influence is very strong, particularly where syntax and vocabulary are concerned; but also in the corruption of certain words, or certain grammatical forms.

Syntax

Direct translations (conscious or subconscious) are to be found in the following peculiarities of speech:

(a) *omission of the relative:* 'a hat is suited' (p.15), 'the man is coming' (p.18), 'with a man killed his father' (p.26), 'her leaky thatch is growing more pasture' (p.33), 'the man bit the yellow lady's nostril' (p.37), 'a crawling beast has passed under a dray' (p.40), 'the young girls would inveigle you off' (p.46), 'it was he did that' (p.50), 'a kind of wonder was jilted' (p.53), 'a man is going to make a marriage' (p.61), 'a man did slay his da' (p.68), 'there's the lad thought he'd rule the roost' (p.71).

(b) *subordinate clause with 'and', but no finite verb:* 'and I piling the turf with the dogs barking' (p.18), 'and I walking forward facing hog, dog or divil' (p.25), 'and you walking the world' (p.28), 'and you without a white shift' (p.42), 'and she with the divil's own temper' (p.47), 'and he a lier on walls' (p.50), 'May I meet him with one tooth and it aching' (p.53), 'and I doing nothing but telling stories' (p.57), and you nothing at all' (p.70), 'and they rhyming songs and ballads' (p.76).

(c) *the imperative formed with 'let':* 'let you not be tempting me' (p.19), 'let you come up then to the fire' (p.21), 'let you stop a short while' (p.26), 'let you be wary' (p.34), 'let you tell us your story' (p.39), 'let you not take it badly' (p.47), 'let you give him a good vengeance' (p.52), 'let you not be putting him in mind of him (p.58), 'let you wait to hear me talking' (p.64), 'let you take it, Pegeen Mike' (p.74).

(d) *I'm after doing, that is, I have just done:* 'I'm after feeling' (p.17), 'And I after toiling, moiling' (pp.29–30), 'I'm after meeting Shawn Keogh' (p.31), 'What's that she's after saying?' (p.34), 'and we after rising early' (p.37), 'And I after holding out' (p.50), 'and he after bringing bankrupt ruin' (p.56), 'and he after doing nothing' (p.70), 'you're after making a mighty man of me' (p.72).

(e) *certain inversions:* 'Isn't it long the nights are now?' (p.16), 'you'd be going is it?' (p.20), 'the like of a king, is it?' (p.29), 'And it's that you'd call sport, is it?' (p.30), 'This night is it?' (p.32), 'is it you's the man killed his father?' (p.38), 'It's bona fides by the road they are' (p.43), 'It's making game of me you were' (p.45), 'Torment him is it?' (p.50), 'Is it mad you's are?' (p.61), 'And it's lies you told' (p.70).

(f) *emphatic forms:* 'He is surely' (p.16), 'You'll not, surely' (p.17), 'I am not, Michael James' (p.18), 'I did not, mister' (p.23), 'You would, surely' (p.26), 'If they are itself' (p.28), 'Not the girls itself' (p.29), 'The divil a one' (p.30), 'She did not' (p.32), 'Faith I wont' (p.34), 'I am, God help me' (p.38), 'There was not' (p.43), 'if she scratched itself' (p.47), 'or if he did itself' (p.51), 'It is, then' (p.59), 'I will not, then', (p.71).

(g) *habitual and progressive tenses with present participle:* 'I'm saying' (p.17), 'I'm thinking' (p.19), 'he'll be having my life' (p.21), 'Is it often the polis *do be* coming into this place?' (p.21), 'the peelers is fearing him' (p.25), 'I'm telling you' (p.28), '*do be* ploughing' (p.36), 'What is it you're wanting?' (p.41), '*do be* looking on the Lord' (p.44), '*do be* passing' (p.50), 'shall be turning again' (p.53), 'I'll be asking God' (p.54), 'you'll be starting' (p.64), 'the times sweet smells *do be* rising' (p.64).

(h) *certain words, phrases and expressions:* have a right to (p.16), have no call to (p.16), the way that (= with the result that) (*passim*), boreen, loy, poteen, cleeve, curragh, shebeen, banbh, frish-frash, streeleen, streeler, thraneen, cnuceen.

(i) *future after 'when':* 'when the sun'll be rising' (p.27), 'when the cocks will crow' (p.34).

Moreover there are a number of corruptions: 'riz' for 'raised' (p.24), 'divil' for devil (*passim*), 'spavindy' for 'spavined' (p.53), 'parlatic' for 'paralytic' (p.62), 'darlint' for 'darling' (p.63), 'drownded' for 'drowned' (p.67), 'gallous' for 'gallows' (= fine) (p.74); and a number of grammatical perversions: 'seen' for 'saw' (very frequent), 'hurted' for 'hurt', 'bit' for 'bitten', 'rose' for 'risen'; 'the men *is* coming', '*them* stories', 'the peelers *is* fearing him', '*near* got six months', '*them's* his boots', '*them* tweeds', 'the airs *is* warming'.

Notice also the frequent use of 'for to' for 'to' – a survival of Elizabethan English, incorrect today. All these variations from normal English mean that the language of the play is distinctive and unusual.

Poetry

Other features add to its poetry, for instance constant alliteration and onomatopoeia, the use of effective epithets, the evocative function of proper names.

Alliteration occurs right through the play, so a few examples will suffice: 'walking off to wakes or weddings' (p.16), 'stony, scattered fields, or scribes of bog' (p.28), 'lead that lad forward for to lodge with me' (p.32), 'Drink a health to the wonders of the western world . . . peelers' (p.41), 'with one blow to the breeches belt' (p.49), 'shooting out his sheep's eyes' (p.51), 'rats as big as badgers sucking the life-blood from the butt of my lug' (p.62), 'making mighty kisses with our wetted mouths' (p.64), 'I'd liefer live a bachelor' (p.68), 'a great gap between a gallous story and a dirty deed' (p.74).

Examples of onomatopoeia, or the use of words whose sound suggests the sense, are frequently to be found. These may relate to farm animals: 'the cows breathing and sighing in the stillness of the air' (p.16), 'slit the windpipe of a screeching sow' (p.24); to wild nature: 'a rabbit starting to screech' (p.30), 'pacing Neifin in the dews of night (p.64), 'the madmen of Keel, eating muck and green weeds on the faces of the cliffs' (p.75); or to people: 'let you step off nimble' (p.27), 'I'd hear himself snoring out – a loud, lonesome snore' (p.30), 'talking whispers at the fall of night' (p.43), 'a girl you'd see itching and scratching' (p.53). Or again, they may reinforce an effective image: 'your whole skin needing washing like a Wicklow sheep' (p.26), 'shying clods against the visage of the stars' (p.30), 'digging spuds in his cold, sloping, stony, divil's patch of a field' (p.39), 'lead you short cuts through the Meadows of Ease, and up the floor of Heaven to the Footstool of the Virgin's Son' (p.54). Other noticeable appeals to the ear are the use of tautology: 'little, small feet', 'every female woman', 'one only son', 'next and nighest', 'one single blow', 'a female wife'; the evocation of religious names in many different situations and the pleasant sound of place names.

Finally it has been pointed out that there are many 'concealed' lines of poetry, either blank verse or alexandrines:

(a) *blank verse:*

'I'll maybe tell them, and I'll maybe not' (p.18)
'That God in Glory may be thanked for that!' (p.34)
'I'll bet my dowry that he'll lick the world' (p.39)
'I seen him raving on the sands today' (p.55).

(b) *alexandrines:*

'As naked as an ash-tree in the moon of May' (p.30)
'A hideous fearful villain, and the spit of you' (p.52)
'I felt them making whistles of my ribs within' (p.71)
'I've lost the only Playboy of the Western World' (p.77).

There are many more such lines in the play; with the other features of the language we have exemplified, they add to the poetic beauty of the work where we have so much poetry *without* versification. We may conclude this part by quoting three critics on Synge's language:

'Synge wrote in a prose that sets him high among the poets' (Maurice Bourgeois).

'All the characters speak to the same rhythm and their speech is made up of words and phrases from different parts of the country, with Gaelic idioms authorised and unauthorised' (Padraic Colum).

'He made word and phrase dance to a very strange rhythm, which will always till his plays have created their own tradition, be difficult to actors who have not learned it from his own lips' (W.B. Yeats).

Part 4

Hints for study

IT SHOULD ALWAYS be borne in mind that *The Playboy of the Western World* (like any other play) was written for performance on the stage. Its impact depends primarily on what we see and on what we hear. The words of the characters and the way they express themselves, their gestures, movements, actions and reactions, are therefore highly significant. As a result, the reader, whose only access to the play is through the text, must try to *see* in his mind's eye, imagining what is taking place on the stage; and, by repeating certain chosen speeches or expressions aloud, he must try to appreciate the flavour of the dialogue, the richness of the language. 'In a good play', wrote Synge in his preface, 'every speech should be as fully flavoured as a nut or apple' (p.12). While this way of approach can only be a second best, ideally speaking, a great deal can be learned from a careful reading and a close study of such a classic as *The Playboy*. The purpose of Part 4 is to suggest how the play may be profitably studied, from different aspects, with a view to illuminating its meaning (or meanings) and discovering its significance. With this end in view, a number of possible questions are proposed for detailed study and model answers provided for two of them.

Proposed questions for detailed study

1. 'On the stage one must have reality, and one must have joy' (preface). To what extent does *The Playboy of the Western World* fulfil this requirement?
2. Examine the different levels of comedy in the play.
3. Compare and contrast: Pegeen Mike and the Widow Quin
   Shawn Keogh and the Playboy
   Michael James and Old Mahon.
4. What do we learn from the play about attitudes:
   to religion,
   to politics,
   to the law,
   to the outside world?
5. Discuss the use of irony and satire in the play.
6. Discuss the use of imagery in the play.

Model answers

'On the stage one must have reality, and one must have joy' (preface). To what extent does 'The Playboy of the Western World' fulfil this requirement?

(a) *Reality* However fantastic the story seemed in 1907 (and still seems today), Synge was able to cite the Lynchelaun case, reported in the newspapers at the time; and to refer to the account given him on the Aran Islands of a similar happening. Both these events illustrate the central plot of the play: the sheltering of a parricide by a village community in the west of Ireland. Whatever we may think about the likelihood of such an event, the reality of the context is beyond question, for the play takes place in the north of Co. Mayo, near Belmullet and not far from Castlebar and Ballina. Further south in Co. Kerry, Christy's part of the world, we learn of 'the poets of Dingle Bay' and Shawn Keogh's 'blue bull from Sneem'. To the north, there is the Sligo boat, and the Protestant part of Ireland with its 'holy Luthers'. Dublin, the capital, is evoked by its National Museum full of skulls, and by Kilmainhan Gaol. Beyond the seas is the United States, land of plenty. So the region of the shebeen is firmly rooted geographically; and this is stressed by family names which (to this day) are characteristic of the area, for example, Mahon, Flaherty, Keogh, and Quin. Allusions to contemporary events – the Boer War, agrarian troubles – and to local terms such as 'shebeen', 'boreen', 'poteen', help to make it perfectly clear when and where the action takes place.

The economic and social level of the people and their daily concerns and activities are no less explicit. We hear of bad harvests, of the flight from the land; and we listen to the Widow Quin bargaining, successively with Shawn and the Playboy, for the acquisition of certain agricultural advantages. The former is an acceptable fiancé, not merely because Pegeen's choice is limited, but also because he is a man of substance in the district. Arranged marriages are the rule, Pegeen's short-lived 'love affair' with Christy the exception.

In this remote village, social life is uneventful and demoralising; the influence of the Catholic Church (through the never-seen, but constantly-felt, Father Reilly) crushing; the opportunities for fun and adventure minimal. Thus anything out of the ordinary is welcome and admirable: Jimmy Farrell hanging 'his dog from the licence'; 'the man bit the yellow lady's nostril on the northern shore'; the Playboy with his story of killing his father. Moreover Pegeen's admiration for the acts of violence committed by Daneen Sullivan and Marcus Quin illustrate this tendency, as well as stressing the understandable opposition to law and order of Irish peasants at that time (Act 1). Law and order, such as it was (we remember the 'loosed khaki cut-throats' and the juries 'selling judgements of the English law'), was administered by England, the invader. Bailiffs, agents and landlords were the natural enemies. In sheltering Christy from the peelers, the villagers could easily feel they were acting patriotically.

It is not an accident that the action takes place in a public-house, full of barrels, jugs and bottles; the social centre where the people naturally foregather. Whatever defence may be offered for heavy drinking in Ireland – unfortunate history, depressing climate, lack of social amenities – it is a feature of country life which Synge had observed at close quarters. Both the fathers in the play drink to excess, and in both cases this is presented as an exploit, something to be admired. Synge's realism in this respect was not likely to win him friends; it was too uncomfortably close to the truth.

The veracity of Synge's language was for long hotly contested. Yet in the preface he himself asserts 'I have used one or two words only that I have not heard among the country people of Ireland'; and in fact the play is full of constructions, expressions and words that are characteristic of the kind of English spoken in Ireland (see Part 3).

If Synge's audiences in the early years reacted badly to his picture of the country, with poverty, law-breaking, drunkenness and boasting to the fore, instead of the conventional image of the 'land of saints and scholars', it was partly no doubt because they realised that he was holding the mirror up to nature, reflecting an unpalatable reality.

(b) *Joy* Most of the aspects of reality we have considered are scarcely gay, yet the play is full of laughter and joy. How is this achieved?

First, through comic incidents, which are a delight to the eye: Shawn's hasty departure in Act 1, at the thought of being left alone in the house all night with Pegeen; Pegeen and the Widow Quin tugging at Christy from different sides; Christy trying vainly to hide the looking-glass from the village girls; Christy seeing his 'assassinated' father arriving; Old Mahon's third return and the public humiliation of his boastful son; the former's fourth return on all fours, 'to be killed a third time'.

Second, through joyful, colourful descriptions, which are at opposite poles from the 'joyless and pallid words' with which Synge taxes Ibsen* and Zola† in his preface: Christy describing the violent, drunken behaviour of his father, 'as naked as an ash-tree in the moon of May' (p.30), or portraying the widow his father had chosen to be his wife, 'a walking terror from beyond the hills (p.40); Old Mahon describing

*Hendrik Ibsen (1828–1906), the Norwegian dramatist.
†Emile Zola (1840–1902), the French novelist.

Christy's terror of the girls, 'shooting out his sheep's eyes between the little twigs and the leaves' (p.51), or his own fits of madness (p.62); Michael James holding forth on marriage and celibacy (p.69); Pegeen denouncing the scandalous conduct of the Widow Quin, 'Doesn't the world know you reared a black ram at your own breast?' (p.33); the mule race as depicted through the window of the shebeen.

Third, through the love scenes, which, in their innocent simplicity and their poetic beauty, fill us with gladness and gaiety, even though each of these three scenes (one in each act) is interrupted by a burlesque incident.

Maybe this joy, which is never long absent from the play, corresponds to a need to react against a restrictive social environment, a history of oppression and defeat, a narrow and powerful Church. Whatever the explanation, it would be difficult to query its existence or remain indifferent to its charm. While the play has been appreciated for a variety of reasons down the years – creative imagination, remarkable dramatic construction, highly individual characters, superb poetic language – the overall impression is one of a slice of life, strikingly realistic yet imbued with laughter and joy.

Examine the different levels of comedy in the play

In his preface to another of his plays, *The Tinker's Wedding*, Synge wrote: 'Of the things which nourish the imagination humour is one of the most needful, and it is dangerous to limit or destroy it.' In this sense, we have a veritable feast in *The Playboy of the Western World* where humour is unrestricted, joyous and free. How does the dramatist achieve his comic effects and what is the nature of his humour?

A study of the levels of comedy in *The Playboy* will show exceptional range, from broad farce to subtle irony. Let us consider these levels, play in hand.

(a) *Farce* Synge does not disdain the effects of farce on the stage, the primitive appeal to eye and ear, which transcends nationality and education, and is to be found in the greatest comic writers: Cervantes (1547–1616), the Spanish author who created the character Don Quixote, Shakespeare (1564–1616), the English poet and dramatist, and Molière (1622–1673), the greatest of French comic dramatists. Indeed it is likely that his close acquaintance with the plays of Shakespeare and Molière encouraged him to include so many farcical scenes in his own comedies. While a number of such scenes appeal at different levels, it is worth trying to separate farce from less elementary forms of humour.

There seems to be a steady increase in the number of farcical scenes as the play progresses, perhaps because Christy's arrival at the shebeen and his fabulous tale have laid the foundations for absurd behaviour and extravagant language. At all events, there are only two really ludicrous scenes in the first act: Shawn Keogh leaving his coat in Michael James's hands; and, later, Pegeen and the Widow Quin tussling over Christy. While there are undertones of subtler comedy on each occasion (Shawn's subservience to Father Reilly, women fighting over a man) the immediate appeal is primitive and visual: an undignified physical situation.

In Act 2 there are more such scenes: Sara putting on Christy's boots; Christy desperately trying to conceal the looking-glass from the girls; Christy and the Widow Quin drinking with arms linked; Christy wearing Shawn's new clothes; and, best of all, Old Mahon's first appearance, with Christy hiding behind the door. The appeal is still mainly visual in this swift series of comic sketches, though the extravagant, highly-coloured language is a delight to the ear. How can the dramatist go further in this direction, we wonder, as the curtain falls.

Yet he can, and does, in Act 3, where we move from one farcical incident to another at bewildering speed: Jimmy and Philly, slightly drunk, talking nonsense about skulls and bones; Old Mahon's second entrance; Michael James's drunken return from the wake; Shawn Keogh fleeing from Christy's threats of violence; Old Mahon beating his son before the assembled villagers; Sara's petticoat being fastened on Christy; Christy biting Shawn; Pegeen scorching Christy; Old Mahon's last return on all fours.

The Playboy himself is directly involved in most of these scenes. Apart from Synge's obvious delight in farce, such scenes often have a clear dramatic function: the hero is being humiliated and ridiculed as a very proper punishment for his vanity, boasting and lies.

(b) *Reversal of fortune* Very close to farce, but at a slightly higher level of comedy, we have a veritable see-saw of changing situations, chiefly involving the Playboy himself – unexpected, dramatic and very funny. A few examples will suffice to illustrate what is in fact a constant leitmotiv (or dominant recurring theme) in the play: Christy taken down a peg by Pegeen in Act 2 – the hero becomes a pot-boy, Don Juan, a wanted criminal; after the girls' flattery, after Pegeen's response and Shawn's gifts, Christy, magnificently rigged out, boastful and self-confident, is reduced to a terrified, miserable child at the sight of Old Mahon, 'the walking spirit of my murdered da'; towards the end, the valiant Playboy who 'thought he'd rule the roost in Mayo', is triply humiliated, as the petticoat is thrust over his head, the men rope him, and Pegeen scorches his leg. This reversal of fortune is a delight to the eye; but also to the mind, because it is the proper punishment of vanity and boastfulness; or simply because it satisfies the human love of sharp contrast – parricide to hero, hero to beaten child, father to son's slave, and so on.

(c) *Comedy of character* We are equally delighted when the characters behave in a way we have come to expect from their early appearances: Shawn, the poltroon in Act 1, is contemptible in his timidity in Act 2, odious in his cowardice in Act 3; the Widow Quin's self-seeking and good-humoured cynicism is a source of quiet enjoyment throughout; Christy, once he has established himself as a 'wonder', goes from strength to strength in extravagant language; Old Mahon, who has been built up as a madman and an eccentric, fully justifies our expectations in Act 3. When people behave 'in character', then we are amused and, in some way, curiously satisfied.

(d) *Comedy of language* This subject has been partly dealt with in Part 3. Comic descriptions abound, as when Christy describes his father or the Widow Casey, or Old Mahon describes Christy's weaknesses, or Pegeen paints an unflattering portrait of the Widow Quin. More generally, swearing and cursing, the invocation of God and the saints for very ungodly purposes, add to the comic power of the play. Abuse, exaggeration, or curious juxtapositions have a similar effect, while the famous Irish 'bull', or paradox, is not absent: 'Are you coming to be killed a third time?', says Christy to his father on the latter's final return (p.76).

(e) *Irony* At the highest intellectual level, we have the use of irony. This may be inherent in the language, where we find the incongruous linking of holy terms with unholy actions: 'Marcus Quin, God rest him, got six months for maiming ewes and he a great warrant to tell stories of holy Ireland' (p.17); or, again: 'PEGEEN: Is it killed your father? PLAYBOY: With the help of God I did surely and that the Holy Immaculate Mother may intercede for his soul' (p.24).

More generally, the Catholic Church comes in for some hard knocks, whether through the absurd strictness and narrow orthodoxy of Father Reilly, or through the apparent failures of the faithful to understand his teaching. The most contemptible character in the play, Shawn Keogh, is also, outwardly at least, the most pious; whereas the more spirited Pegeen and Widow Quin are prepared to question, even to mock, ecclesiastical authority. 'Stop tormenting me with Father Reilly' (p.17), says Pegeen to Shawn or, again, 'Go on, then, to Father Reilly and let him put you in the holy brotherhoods' (p.27). The Widow Quin shows her independence from the spiritual adviser more sarcastically: 'It isn't fitting, says the priesteen' (p.32). The abundant use of holy names has already been commented on. Sara Tansey's misconception of the function of confession went deeper: 'When you'd be ashamed this place, going up winter and summer with nothing worth while to confess at all' (p.37).

The attitude to excessive drinking is not spared. Old Mahon's descriptions of his own excesses are presented as an exploit (p.62), while Michael James's idea of a good wake is one where 'there were five men, aye, and six men stretched out retching speechless on the holy stones' (p.66).

Finally the double-think of the people's reaction to the law and its apparatus is constantly evoked: 'the peelers is . . . decent, droughty poor fellows' (p.26); 'the juries . . . selling judgements of the English law' (p.41). Law-breaking is often a feat to be admired, respect for the authorities a matter of expediency, rather than of principle.

It should not be concluded that *The Playboy* is a satire on Irish moral life; but the range of comedy has something for all tastes, from broad farce to skilful irony. Very often the different levels of comedy meet and mingle to the delight of all.

Part 5

Suggestions for further reading

The text

J.M. Synge, Collected Works, Volume IV, edited by Ann Saddlemyer, Oxford University Press, London, 1968. This edition has a valuable introduction and full accompanying textual notes, page by page.

The Playboy of the Western World, edited by T.R. Henn, Methuen, London, 1960. This edition has a useful introduction and some helpful notes.

The Playboy of the Western World and Riders to the Sea, Unwin Paperbacks, London, 1979. This is the edition used in these Notes for page references, and is useful for class work.

Other works by J.M. Synge

PROSE

The Aran Islands

In Wicklow, West Kerry and Connemara

J.M. Synge, Collected Works, Volume II, edited by Alan Price, Oxford University Press, London, 1966.

POEMS AND TRANSLATIONS

J.M. Synge, Collected Works, Volume I, edited by Robin Skelton, Oxford University Press, London, 1962.

OTHER PLAYS

In the Shadow of the Glen

Riders to the Sea

The Well of the Saints

The Tinker's Wedding

Deirdre of the Sorrows, in *J.M. Synge, Collected Works*, Volumes III and IV, edited by Ann Saddlemyer, Oxford University Press, London, 1968.

Biography

GREENE, DAVID AND STEPHENS, EDWARD: *J.M. Synge, 1871–1909*, Collier Books, New York, 1961. Despite numerous misprints, provides a full and fairly accurate account of Synge's life.

Criticism and comment

'The Death of Synge' and 'The Bounty of Sweden' in W.B. Yeats, *Autobiographies*, Macmillan, London, 1955.

'J.M. Synge and the Ireland of his Time' in W.B. Yeats, *Essays and Introductions,* Macmillan, London, 1969.

CORKERY, DANIEL: *Synge and Anglo-Irish Literature*, Cork University Press, Cork, 1931.

SADDLEMYER, ANN: *J.M. Synge and Modern Comedy*, Dolmen Press, Dublin, 1968.

Background reading

ELLIS-FERMOR, UNA: *The Irish Dramatic Movement*, Methuen, London, 1939.

ROBINSON, LENNOX: *Ireland's Abbey Theatre: A History 1899–1951*, Sidgwick and Jackson, London, 1951.

The author of th

MARK MORTIMER is a graduate
ing English language and litera
1947, and is now senior lecturer
d'Etudes Politiques (where he cre
and at the Ecole Nationale d'Adm
'maître de conférences associé' at the

He has published articles and reviews
learned journals in France and Ireland, and
extensively in this field. He is at present
critical review of J.M. Synge.

York Notes

CHINUA ACHEB
Things Fall Ap
EDWARD ALB
Who's Afraid
ANONYMOU
Beowulf
Everyman
W. H. AUD
Selected
JANE AU
Emma
Mansf
North
Pers
Pri
Se
SAN

HENRY FIELDING
Joseph Andrews
Tom Jones

F. SCOTT FITZGERALD
Tender is the Night
The Great Gatsby

GUSTAVE FLAUBERT
Madame Bovary

E. M. FORSTER
A Passage to India
Howards End

JOHN FOWLES
The French Lieutenant's Woman

JOHN GALSWORTHY
Strife

MRS GASKELL
North and South

WILLIAM GOLDING
Lord of the Flies
The Spire

OLIVER GOLDSMITH
She Stoops to Conquer
The Vicar of Wakefield

ROBERT GRAVES
Goodbye to All That

GRAHAM GREENE
Brighton Rock
The Heart of the Matter
The Power and the Glory

WILLIS HALL
The Long and the Short and the Tall

THOMAS HARDY
Far from the Madding Crowd
Jude the Obscure
Selected Poems
Tess of the D'Urbervilles
The Mayor of Casterbridge
The Return of the Native
The Woodlanders

L. P. HARTLEY
The Go-Between

NATHANIEL HAWTHORNE
The Scarlet Letter

SEAMUS HEANEY
Selected Poems

ERNEST HEMINGWAY
A Farewell to Arms
The Old Man and the Sea

SUSAN HILL
I'm the King of the Castle

BARRY HINES
Kes

HOMER
The Iliad
The Odyssey

GERARD MANLEY HOPKINS
Selected Poems

TED HUGHES
Selected Poems

ALDOUS HUXLEY
Brave New World

HENRIK IBSEN
A Doll's House

HENRY JAMES
The Portrait of a Lady
Washington Square

BEN JONSON
The Alchemist
Volpone

JAMES JOYCE
A Portrait of the Artist as a Young Man
Dubliners

JOHN KEATS
Selected Poems

PHILIP LARKIN
Selected Poems

D. H. LAWRENCE
Selected Short Stories
Sons and Lovers
The Rainbow
Women in Love

HARPER LEE
To Kill a Mocking-Bird

LAURIE LEE
Cider with Rosie

CHRISTOPHER MARLOWE
Doctor Faustus

HERMAN MELVILLE
Moby Dick

THOMAS MIDDLETON *and*
    WILLIAM ROWLEY
The Changeling

ARTHUR MILLER
A View from the Bridge
Death of a Salesman
The Crucible

JOHN MILTON
Paradise Lost I & II
Paradise Lost IV & IX
Selected Poems

V. S. NAIPAUL
A House for Mr Biswas

ROBERT O'BRIEN
Z for Zachariah

SEAN O'CASEY
Juno and the Paycock

GEORGE ORWELL
Animal Farm
Nineteen Eighty-four

JOHN OSBORNE
  Look Back in Anger
WILFRED OWEN
  Selected Poems
ALAN PATON
  Cry, The Beloved Country
THOMAS LOVE PEACOCK
  Nightmare Abbey and *Crotchet Castle*
HAROLD PINTER
  The Caretaker
SYLVIA PLATH
  Selected Works
PLATO
  The Republic
ALEXANDER POPE
  Selected Poems
J. B. PRIESTLEY
  An Inspector Calls
WILLIAM SHAKESPEARE
  A Midsummer Night's Dream
  Antony and Cleopatra
  As You Like It
  Coriolanus
  Hamlet
  Henry IV Part I
  Henry IV Part II
  Henry V
  Julius Caesar
  King Lear
  Macbeth
  Measure for Measure
  Much Ado About Nothing
  Othello
  Richard II
  Richard III
  Romeo and Juliet
  Sonnets
  The Merchant of Venice
  The Taming of the Shrew
  The Tempest
  The Winter's Tale
  Troilus and Cressida
  Twelfth Night
GEORGE BERNARD SHAW
  Arms and the Man
  Candida
  Pygmalion
  Saint Joan
  The Devil's Disciple
MARY SHELLEY
  Frankenstein
PERCY BYSSHE SHELLEY
  Selected Poems
RICHARD BRINSLEY SHERIDAN
  The Rivals

R. C. SHERRIFF
  Journey's End
JOHN STEINBECK
  Of Mice and Men
  The Grapes of Wrath
  The Pearl
LAURENCE STERNE
  A Sentimental Journey
  Tristram Shandy
TOM STOPPARD
  Professional Foul
  Rosencrantz and Guildenstern are Dead
JONATHAN SWIFT
  Gulliver's Travels
JOHN MILLINGTON SYNGE
  The Playboy of the Western World
TENNYSON
  Selected Poems
W. M. THACKERAY
  Vanity Fair
J. R. R. TOLKIEN
  The Hobbit
MARK TWAIN
  Huckleberry Finn
  Tom Sawyer
VIRGIL
  The Aeneid
ALICE WALKER
  The Color Purple
KEITH WATERHOUSE
  Billy Liar
EVELYN WAUGH
  Decline and Fall
JOHN WEBSTER
  The Duchess of Malfi
OSCAR WILDE
  The Importance of Being Earnest
THORNTON WILDER
  Our Town
TENNESSEE WILLIAMS
  The Glass Menagerie
VIRGINIA WOOLF
  Mrs Dalloway
  To the Lighthouse
WILLIAM WORDSWORTH
  Selected Poems
WILLIAM WYCHERLEY
  The Country Wife
W. B. YEATS
  Selected Poems

York Handbooks: list of titles

YORK HANDBOOKS form a companion series to York Notes and are designed to meet the wider needs of students of English and related fields. Each volume is a compact study of a given subject area, written by an authority with experience in communicating the essential ideas to students at all levels.

AN INTRODUCTORY GUIDE TO ENGLISH LITERATURE
by MARTIN STEPHEN
PREPARING FOR EXAMINATIONS IN ENGLISH LITERATURE
by NEIL McEWAN
READING THE SCREEN
An Introduction to Film Studies
by JOHN IZOD
ENGLISH POETRY
by CLIVE T. PROBYN
ENGLISH USAGE
by COLIN G. HEY
ENGLISH GRAMMAR
by LORETO TODD
AN INTRODUCTION TO LINGUISTICS
by LORETO TODD
AN INTRODUCTION TO LITERARY CRITICISM
by RICHARD DUTTON
A DICTIONARY OF LITERARY TERMS
by MARTIN GRAY
STUDYING CHAUCER
by ELISABETH BREWER
STUDYING SHAKESPEARE
by MARTIN STEPHEN *and* PHILIP FRANKS
STUDYING JANE AUSTEN
by IAN MILLIGAN
STUDYING THE BRONTËS
by SHEILA SULLIVAN
STUDYING CHARLES DICKENS
by K. J. FIELDING
STUDYING THOMAS HARDY
by LANCE ST JOHN BUTLER
A CHRONOLOGY OF ENGLISH LITERATURE
by MARTIN GRAY
A DICTIONARY OF BRITISH AND IRISH AUTHORS
by ANTONY KAMM
AN A.B.C. OF SHAKESPEARE
by P. C. BAYLEY
THE METAPHYSICAL POETS
by TREVOR JAMES
THE AGE OF ROMANTIC LITERATURE
by HARRY BLAMIRES